Puff Adder
The puff adder's camouflaged skin helps it hide in the sand while waiting to strike.

substance that fingernails are made of.

Milk snake
The harmless Sinaloan milk snake fools predators because it looks like the highly venomous coral snake.

Red-footed Tortoise
This tortoise gets its name because some of the scales on its feet are bright red.

Horned Viper
The horns of this venomous viper are made of tough scales and make it look frightening.

Flying Snake

Flying snakes can't really fly. They flatten their bodies to glide through the air.

11

Hognose Viper

This is one of the smallest poisonous snakes in the world.

12

Nile Crocodile

Nile crocodiles sometimes hunt in groups. They surround their prey, latch onto its body, and twist their bodies to rip it apart.

13

14

Green Iguana

An iguana uses its tail as a rudder for swimming. If someone grabs its tail, it breaks off, leaving the iguana free to swim to safety.

Snake-necked Turtle

The snake-necked turtle has two defenses— a very hard shell and the ability to give off a nasty smell to drive predators away.

15

Cook's Tree Boa
A boa uses the front half of its body to squeeze prey to death, while its tail holds on to a tree branch.

Burmese Python
Pythons can grow to over 30 feet (9 meters) long and live for more than 20 years.

This stream brings fresh rainwater from the mountains.

Indian Cobra
This venomous snake spreads out the skin on its neck when it is ready to attack.

Water Dragon
Water dragons drop out of trees or race into the water to hide from danger. They can stay underwater for up to 30 minutes.

Spectacled Caiman
A caiman is an alligator, not a crocodile. The bony ridges above its eyes make it look like it's wearing spectacles.

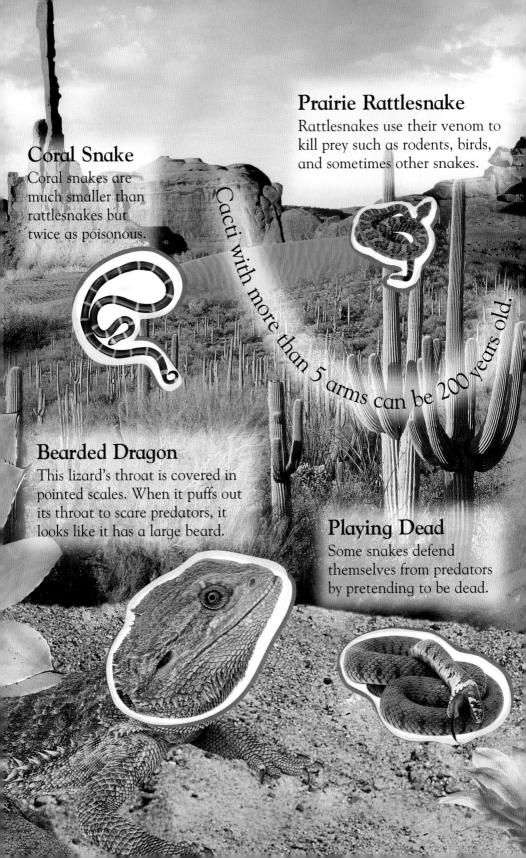

Coral Snake
Coral snakes are much smaller than rattlesnakes but twice as poisonous.

Prairie Rattlesnake
Rattlesnakes use their venom to kill prey such as rodents, birds, and sometimes other snakes.

Cacti with more than 5 arms can be 200 years old.

Bearded Dragon
This lizard's throat is covered in pointed scales. When it puffs out its throat to scare predators, it looks like it has a large beard.

Playing Dead
Some snakes defend themselves from predators by pretending to be dead.

Rattlesnake
Rattlesnakes rattle their tails when they feel threatened as a warning to predators.

Thai Cobra
This dangerous snake kills hundreds of people every year.

Southern Pacific Rattlesnake
Rattlesnakes hunt using heat sensors on the sides of their heads. They can find prey that is only one tenth of a degree warmer than their surroundings.

Sandfish
These skinks bury themselves in the sand, eat insects, and have a painful bite.

Rain forest

There are five main types of reptiles—
snakes, lizards, turtles, crocodiles, and the
tuatara. The scaly skin of reptiles doesn't keep in
body heat, so reptiles rely on the warmth of their
surroundings, like this rain forest, to keep warm.
In a rain forest you might find an anaconda, the
largest snake on earth, or a chameleon, a lizard
that can change color to match its habitat.

Basilisk

Basilisks like warm, wet forests
where they can run, swim, and
climb trees. They can even run
across the surface of the water.

New Guinea Ground Boa

Pythons, boas, and
anacondas are all
constrictors—they
kill their prey by
squeezing it to death

Indian Python

The Indian python is an arboreal
snake, which means that it
lives mainly in trees.

Egg-eating snake

A snake swallows its prey whole
and digests it in its stomach.

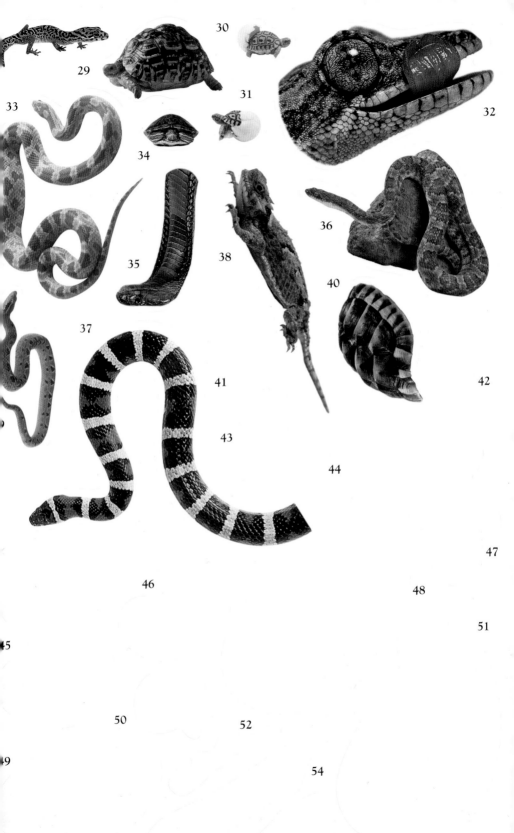

29

30

31

32

33

34

35

36

37

38

40

41

42

43

44

45

46

47

48

49

50

51

52

53

54

Jackson's Chameleon

A chameleon's skin changes color to match its surroundings. Its eyeballs can also move in every direction, which gives it 360-degree vision.

23

24

Mangrove Snake

This snake is a fast and graceful climber and usually does not leave the trees.

25

Wood Turtle

Each bump on the shell of a wood turtle is covered in rings like the cross-section of a branch. Wood turtles can live for 58 years.

26

Crocodile

Crocodiles have thinner snouts than alligators. A crocodile's lower teeth can be seen when its mouth is shut, but when an alligator closes its mouth, its teeth are hidden.

27

Desert Reptiles

Cold-blooded creatures such as reptiles don't need to eat very often to maintain their body temperature like warm-blooded humans do. They do need the sun's heat to keep warm though, so a warm place without much food, such as a desert can be a perfect home. Some of the world's most deadly snakes and scariest-looking lizards live here, hiding under rocks, in abandoned houses, in long dry grass, and in trees.

Banded Gecko

Geckos are small lizards that are usually active at night. This gecko can live off the fat stored in its tail for nine months. If the gecko is grabbed by its tail, the tail breaks off—but it always grows back.

28

30

29

31

32

Leopard Tortoise

A mother leopard tortoise will bury up to 30 eggs in the ground. Her babies wont hatch for a whole year.

Bath Time

Some lizards clean their eyes by licking them with their long tongues.

Corn Snake

This non-poisonous snake gets its name because the markings on its belly look like the pattern of kernels on an ear of corn.

33

In some deserts it might not rain for a whole year.

Turtle or Tortoise?

Turtles have webbed feet and spend most of their lives in water. Tortoises live on land and have stumpy feet to help them walk.

34

35

Lyre Snake

The lyre snake's narrow neck makes its wide head look like a triangle.

36

Spitting Cobra

This snake spits venom up to 8 feet (2.5 meters) as a defense, but kills by injecting venom with its teeth.

Anaconda
The anaconda is
the largest snake
in the world.

20

Many brightly colored animals live in the rain forest.

Copperhead
The bite of a North American
copperhead snake is venomous,
but rarely fatal to humans.

21

22

Rainbow Boa
When sunlight strikes the
rainbow boa, its skin shines
with the colors of the rainbow.

Lancehead
This venomous snake lives in tropical South America.

16

Red-tailed Racer
The red-tailed racer is a harmless snake that lives in forests such as the Khao Soke rain forest in Thailand.

17

Tuatara
Tuataras are the last survivors of their family of reptiles. They are only found on the coasts of New Zealand.

18

Viperine Snake
The viperine is an aquatic snake found near ponds and rivers. It preys on fish and amphibians.

19

King Snake
The brightly colored king snake is harmless to humans.

37

38

Horned Lizard
Horned lizards, also known as horned toads because of their toadlike bodies, warm up in the morning sun and hide in shrubs during the hot day.

39

Pit Viper
Desert vipers bury themselves in the sand to escape the heat. If they are disturbed, they inflict a highly venomous bite.

40

Desert Tortoise
Adult tortoises can survive more than a year without water.